Angie Wonders:
Microscope Fun!

Angie Wonders

Microscope Fun!

Renee Winters

Illustrated by Resky Sutra

Positive Energy
Publishing

Angie Wonders

Microscope Fun!

Published 2020 by Positive Energy Publishing
Publishing Contact: 516-650-9745
Printed in the United States of America

ISBN:9798642349403
First Printing, 2020
Address all inquiries to:
Renee Winters
Email: ms.reneewinters@gmail.com
For book orders visit www.angiewonders.com

*This book is dedicated
to my family,
my source of love and
support.*

Dear Parents,

Thank you for taking this journey with Angie Wonders as she explores the amazing world around her. This series of picture books was created out of my genuine love for my daughter, science, and education. As a veteran educator, it has always been essential to me to be a lifelong learner. This philosophy was always something I worked to instill in my children.

As I explored the areas of science, I realized that there was a deficit of women working in the areas of STEM (Science, Technology, Engineering, and Math). Many of our girls do not see themselves as scientist or inventors. However, this perception can be altered by early exposure. When my daughter was little, I loved when she would ask questions about science and exploration!

As parents, we work to expose our children to various modalities of learning. A picture book is just one of these methods. However, in the *Angie Wonders* book series, there will be questions, fun facts, or even experiments to share with your daughter. The character of Angie Wonders will hopefully help your little girl to imagine, wonder, and question the world around them.

Get ready to explore and be more!

Renee Winters

Angie is so excited today.

More thrilled than ever before.

Her Mommy has bought her something, she saw it at the store.

She kept looking out the window, waiting for the mail to arrive.
It was supposed to be delivered today.
On her porch by five.

So, Angie sat on down and placed a pillow on the steps.
She kept an eye on her watch. It wasn't five yet.

As she passed the time, a beautiful butterfly fluttered at her nose.

She even saw a brown ant moving near her toes. She laughed and giggled as she began to explore. All the creepy moving bugs right outside her door.

Just as she picked up a little curly bug.
She felt her shirt being pulled; she felt a little tug.
It was her Daddy, pointing down the street.
She looked up, smiled, and jumped to her feet.

So excited, so thrilled, "It's here, it's here!"
"Open the box!" she yelled and cheered.

Her microscope was beautiful,
as it sat there on the floor.
It will help her answer questions,
help her to explore.

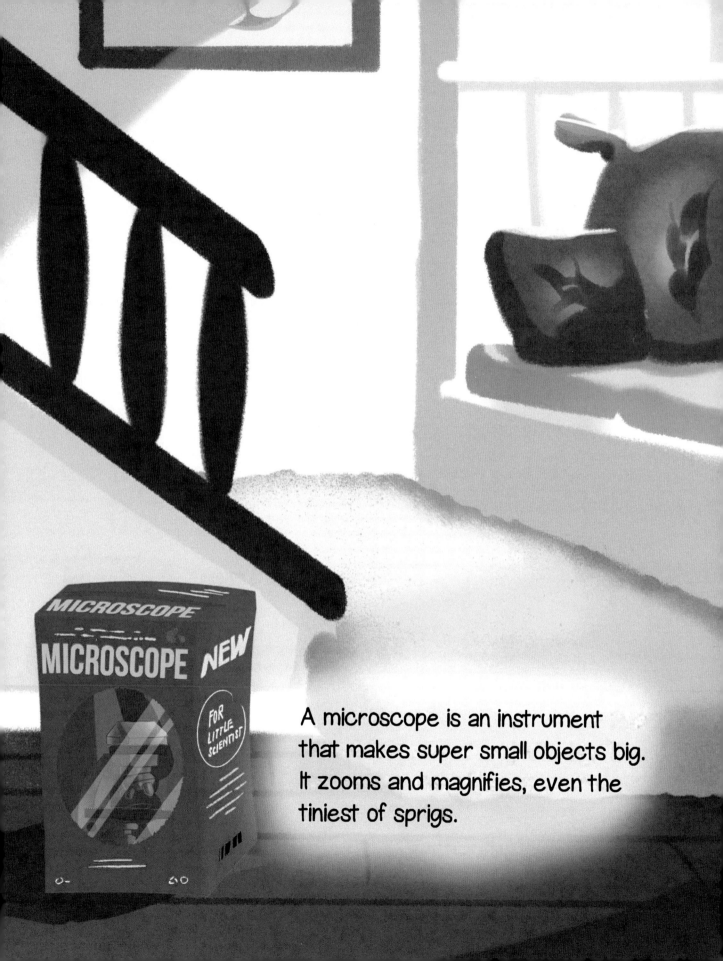

A microscope is an instrument that makes super small objects big. It zooms and magnifies, even the tiniest of sprigs.

Her Mommy helped her read the directions, to set it up just right. It now sat on the table, under the kitchen light.

What was her first object? What would it be?
A cat's whisker, a feather, or maybe dad's old key.
Some salt, a string, or even that gray fuzzy thing.
There were so many things to examine; she wanted them all.
So, she began to make a list of items as she walked down her hall.

She found a shoebox and an old notebook too.
She wanted to keep track of all the things she would use.
After she gathered her items, her heart began to soar.
She ran back to the kitchen, ready to explore.

As she sat at the table looking in her new tool, her first
item was a leaf that she had found in school.
She looked at the lines that she had not seen before.
She couldn't believe her eyes; she wanted to see more.

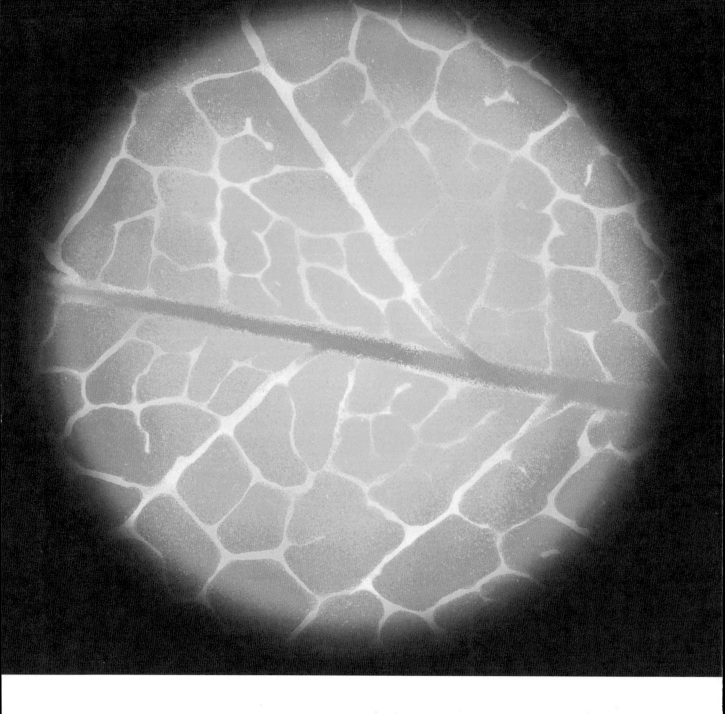

The leaf looked like one of Daddy's road maps, lots of lines
everywhere. So many lines that she didn't know were there.
She couldn't contain her excitement; she looked with disbelief.
Her Mommy explained that she had viewed the plant cells of the leaf.

It was amazing what she saw as she looked in her new microscope.
All the details that she could now see.
A new world had been unlocked, and her microscope was the key.
Knowing she could look closer at objects filled her with joy.
"It's a tool to look at my world; mommy said,
it's more than just a toy."

As darkness began to fall outside the kitchen window,
Angie rubbed her eyes.
She examined so many items, and each offered its surprise.

But she knew it was time for bed
as she walked across her floor.
She glanced back at her
microscope as she closed her
bedroom door.

She jumped in her bed, feeling so free.
Her microscope is fantastic, so many new things to see.
She waited for her Mommy to tuck her in just right.
She closed her eyes just for a moment
but fell asleep in the moonlight.

Angie's Activities

15 Things You Should Look At Under A Microscope

feathers

hair

yarn

salt

sugar

onion skin

leaf

sand

bird seed

thread

lint

grass

parts of a flower

celery fibers

finger nail clippings

My Notes...

My Notes...

_____

_____

_____

_____

_____

_____

_____

_____

_____

_____

Microscope Slides

Draw What You See!

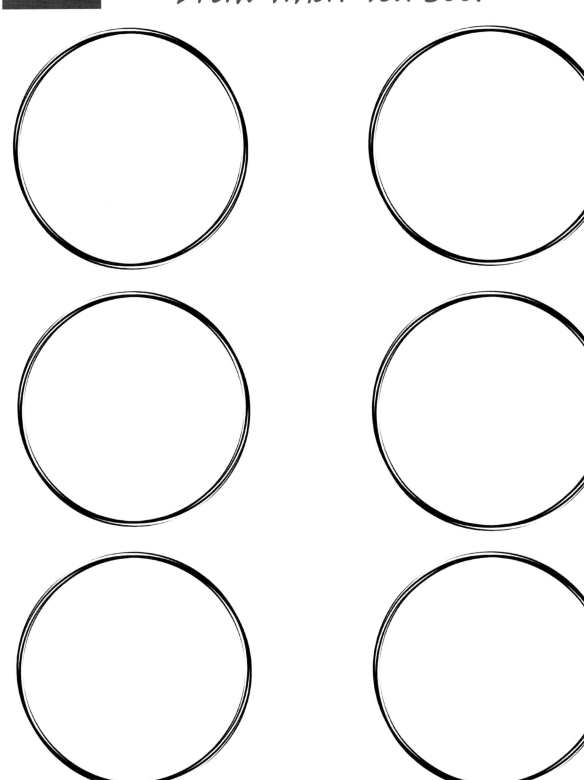

Microscope Slides

Draw What You See!

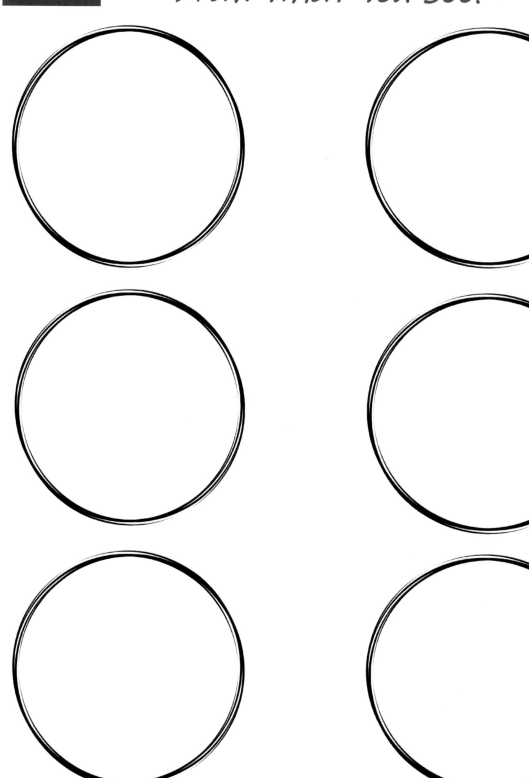